LISTEN/ÉIST:

DOCUMENTARY THEATRE MONOLOGUES FROM *THE GATHERING: COLLECTED ORAL HISTORIES OF THE IRISH IN MONTANA*

Edited by Bernadette Sweeney and Anna Dulba-Barnett

Devised by Cohen Ambrose, Anna Dulba-Barnett, Leah Joki, Reid Reimers, Rebecca Schaffer, Bernadette Sweeney and Sam Williamson

Created by the School of Theatre and Dance, College of Visual and Performing Arts, in partnership with *The Gathering: Collected Oral Histories of the Irish in Montana,* Irish Studies Program, Dept. of English, College of Arts and Sciences, University of Montana.

The University of Montana

Copyright © 2013 Bernadette Sweeney c/o The University of Montana Press
Missoula, MT 59812

All rights reserved. No part of this book may be reproduced by any means without permission of the copyright holder and The University of Montana Press.

For information contact:
The University of Montana Press
Gerald Fetz
International Programs
The University of Montana
32 Campus Drive
Missoula, MT 59812
fetzga@mso.umt.edu

Design: Shauna Murphy - UM Printing & Graphics

Printed in the USA by
The University of Montana Printing & Graphics Services - Missoula, MT
ISBN-978-0-9815760-9-1

— to the Irish of Montana, past, present, and future.

LISTEN/ÉIST was first performed at the Masquer Theatre at the University of Montana School of Theatre and Dance on Dec. 15th 2011.

Director: **Bernadette Sweeney**
Technical design: **Patrick Cook** and **Brandon Woodard**.
Roles in the original production as follows, in order of appearance:

Bob Whaley:
interviewed, devised and performed
by Cohen Ambrose

Ann Cecelia Backstrom:
interviewed, devised and performed
by Leah Joki

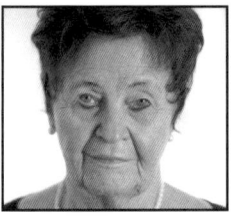

Jeanne Joki Tanner:
interviewed, devised and performed
by Leah Joki

Kris Roberts:
interviewed, devised and performed
by Leah Joki

Joslyn Carney:
interviewed, devised and performed
by Leah Joki

©Photographs by Brandon Woodard and Patrick Cook/*The Gathering*

Colleen Galvin Holzheimer:
interviewed, devised and performed by Rebecca Schaffer

James (Jim) Bullock:
interviewed, devised and performed by Sam Williamson

Johanna Prindiville:
interviewed, devised and performed by Anna Dulba-Barnett

Valerie Danby-Smith:
interviewed, devised and performed by Rebecca Schaffer

Kevin Shannon:
interviewed by Bernadette Sweeney, devised and performed by Reid Reimers

INTRODUCTION

Listen/Éist is an original performance script developed from interview materials collected by *The Gathering*. *Listen/Éist* was created by students of the School of Theatre and Dance at the University of Montana. *The Gathering: Collected Oral Histories of the Irish in Montana* is a long-term interdisciplinary oral history project which records and archives the Irish and Irish American folk histories, memories, practices and traditions of Montana. It is grant supported by the Irish Government Department of Foreign Affairs Emigrant Support Programme and is the research project of the Irish Studies Program at the University of Montana. The project is substantially supported by the University of Montana College of Arts and Sciences (CAS), and this performance project represents a collaboration between CAS and the University of Montana's College of Visual and Performing Arts.

The Gathering: Collected Oral Histories of the Irish in Montana documents the extraordinary historical links between Montana and Ireland. Towards the end of the nineteenth century many Irish miners came from the copper mine in Allihies, West Cork, to the mines of Butte. Cavan-native Marcus Daly, as one of the Copper Kings of Butte, drew many Irish to Montana and, although Butte's mining community was multi-ethnic at the turn of the twentieth century, the Irish were in the undisputed majority. This led to the development or presence of many Irish organizations in Butte such as the Friendly Sons of Saint Patrick, and the Ancient Order of Hibernians. More crucially, however, this led to the presence of many Irish-born laborers in Butte and in other cities across Montana, such as Anaconda and Helena. Subsequent generations moved across the state but held fast to their Irish roots. Others came to Montana not to mine necessarily but to work as ranch hands, laundresses, nurses, smelter-workers, priests, teachers etc. The aims of this oral history project are to document Irish-Montana through recorded audio and video interviews, and to make these interviews available to the public, to scholars and community members, through the Mansfield Library at the University of Montana. We have collected over 170 interviews to date across the state of Montana and in Ireland, and have generated video and audio material, radio, theatre and exhibition material. We aim to generate further publications, conferences, performances, exhibitions and a documentary film based on the project.

Our interviews document Irish performance traditions such as that of the Wrenboy being performed in Butte, stories of Irish laborers, ranchers and miners, emigration histories, religious practices, memories of Irish language in the home, original mining and labor songs, and Irish traditional music. Examples include Frank Gary's story of his mother witnessing the death of her father in a land-war in Mayo in the 1920s, 98-year-old Sarah B. O' Donnell's story of being born in Butte in 1913 but, on the death of her mother in childbirth, being brought back to Carndonagh Co. Donegal to be raised by her grandparents, John 'the Yank' Harrington's first hand memories of the Black and Tan atrocities in west Cork, and many other compelling stories, some of which are included here. *Listen/Éist* includes a cross-section of our material, stories of first or second generation Irish Montanans are told alongside the stories of emigrants from Ireland to Montana [1].

In 2011, I, Bernadette Sweeney, a professor of theatre as well as founder and Head of Research for *The Gathering,* offered a class where students could explore the art of documentary theatre. Documentary theatre, often also referred to as verbatim theatre, is a form of theatre where performance scripts are developed based on transcripts of interviews with members of a particular group, or people who have been affected by a particular issue or event. Other materials can also be used such as court transcripts or newspaper articles. These people are not fictionalized but performed by the actors who work to stage not just their subjects' stories, but their physicality, intonation, vocal expressions etc. For *Listen/Éist* each student conducted interviews with *Gathering* participants across Montana on their Irish heritage and Irish/American identity. These students then transcribed the interviews and selected materials that became the foundation of the script for performance, staged at the Masquer Theatre at the University of Montana, Missoula in December 2011 and in Butte, Montana in March 2012.

This script is made up of extracts from ten interviews which capture the local stories of the Montana Irish, including those from a working mother in Butte, a railway worker in Great Falls, and a singer and storyteller who brought about changes in the state legislation for the mentally disabled. These stories are affecting, funny, tragic, and heartfelt. What is especially compelling about these pieces is the intimacy with which they are told — the play has an impact precisely because of the recorded hesitations, breaths, pauses, and accent of each storyteller. In this way the stories come alive for the spectator, and for the reader.

Listen/Éist provides one example of how we can remember the forgotten or silent voices of the emigrant (and subsequent) generations and create an opportunity for them to be heard again. The actors quite literally gave voice to these stories in performance, performing first or second hand accounts of the experience of being Irish Montanan, of the cultural shifts, the leave-taking, and the work to settle into a new environment without forgetting what was so defining about the old. *Listen/ Éist* (*Éist* being the Irish or Gaelic word for listen) is so called as this performance piece is precisely that — a call for us as audience members, as interviewers, or as community members to remember to listen to the voices of those whose experiences have shaped them, have shaped us, and those around us. In this instance we examine the stories of Montana's Irish and the Irish emigrant experience, but these stories could be those of many cultures or ethnicities, and they remind us of the importance of remembering, and valuing the stories of our forebears, our friends, ourselves — they remind us to listen.

Missoula native Bob Whaley was interviewed by Cohen Ambrose. As the project progressed it was uncanny how Ambrose seemed to resemble his older subject more and more. Whaley tells many stories over the course of his interview with Ambrose, and again the selection process was difficult. Because these seemed neatly episodic, we broke them into sections and used Ambrose's performance as a framing device for the overall performance. Whaley's stories ranged from his Irish American heritage and identity, to growing up during World War II in Missoula, to serving as a pilot in the Vietnam War. During his interview with Ambrose, Whaley brought out a document he himself had written in response to his experiences in Vietnam, and Ambrose performed a section of this in *Listen/Éist* (included in this script). What Whaley's interview gives us is the perspective of the Irish American experience as part of the greater American experience, of Irishness as one ethnicity among so very many, which are all also American.

One graduate student, Leah Joki, is a native of Butte and for her piece she interviewed four generations of her family. She was lucky to have in her possession a video interview she had recorded with her grandmother in 1989. This is an extraordinary piece of archival footage in itself. Joki's grandmother, Ann Cecilia Kinsella Backstrom, was a straight-talking, unapologetic and politically incorrect interviewee. Leah had difficulty editing the material down to what was needed for performance, as it was all so rich. Here we saw performed the layers of memory: Leah Joki, a talented actor in her fifties, performed onstage with a large video image of her late grandmother behind her, speaking to Leah's younger self. We deliberately left Joki's questions in the edit of the video material, so we staged her voice and image from 1989, as well as her live voice in 2011. Joki overtly performed alongside this image of her grandmother, replicating her gestures, and voice intonation as she spoke along with her. Video footage was also shown of Joki's mother, sister and niece, but for these Joki sat in stillness, and allowed these stories to give perspective to the story of her grandmother.

Sam Williamson, the only undergraduate student involved in this performance, recorded an interview with James (Jim) Bullock who approached *The Gathering* as he wanted to tell the story of his Irish grandfather. Bullock did that, very precisely, in just over twenty minutes, almost entirely without interruption. Working with the single prop of an unlit cigar, Williamson worked to perform the intonations, expressions and rich humour of a man over fifty years his senior. It was fascinating in rehearsal to work with Williamson to find a slower, more grounded physicality and voice — a real challenge for this lively and energetic young performer. Interestingly, as director, I found the points of access to be the voice and the gestures with the cigar — these helped Williamson to find the maturity of his interviewee without losing Bullock's older energy and drive to remember this profound figure in his life, his Irish grandfather.

Anna Dulba-Barnett interviewed one of the participants in *The Gathering: Collected Oral Histories of the Irish in Montana* who came directly from Ireland. Johanna Prindiville came to America with her family at the age of eleven. Dulba-Barnett chose to stage Prindiville's recorded voice as well as perform it, and spoke sections of the interviewee's dialogue in tandem with a recording of that section in Prindiville's own voice. The audience could thereby hear the two voices overlap to mark transitions, then Prindiville's voice would fade out and the actor's would continue. Prindiville's interview offers us a very raw recounting of the experience of emigration from the perspective of a child.

Rebecca Schaffer chose a different challenge in that she chose to perform two subjects, Colleen Galvin Holzheimer of Great Falls, Montana and Valerie Danby-Smith, Irish-born but living in Bozeman Montana. Schaffer used a technique that has been brought to the fore of verbatim theatre by Recorded Delivery Theatre Company of the UK [2]. This technique is to play a recording during the performance that only the actor can hear through an earpiece. The actor listens to the subject's interview material live in the performance moment, and speaks the interviewee's words at a time-lag of about three to five seconds. This obviously requires a lot of skill on the part of the actor and a very high level of familiarity with the material, but the advantages are that the actor is reminded of the nuancing and phrasing of the interviewee in the moment of performance [3]. For her work with Danby-Smith's material Schaffer chose to focus on the details of Danby-Smith's Irish childhood, and her emphasis on the magical and the mythical elements of the Irish landscape and folklore. Schaffer had taken some beautiful photographs of her second interviewee, Great Falls native Colleen Galvin Holzheimer, and these became central to her performance of this other story. These images, coupled with Galvin Holzheimer's levels of personal interest and historical research made for some very rich material as she focused her interview on the story of her grandmother. These different emphases by Schaffer, coupled with the recorded voices through her earpiece, allowed her to differentiate clearly between these two subjects, and do full justice to both of their stories.

Finally, Reid Reimers performed Kevin Shannon, a Butte native and son of an emigrant from Miltown-Malbay in County Clare. Reimers had conducted a number of very strong interviews but, as he himself is a talented singer, he asked if he could work with something from our collection that included song. He performed Butte-native Kevin Shannon. Shannon's father was a native of Miltown Malbay Co. Clare and Shannon has a very strong connection to his Irish heritage as a singer and storyteller. Reimers made the choice to stage Shannon as both the older, somewhat infirm man as interviewed, and a stronger, more vibrant, younger version, and used the songs to transition between the two. Shannon's interview covered his singing and storytelling, and documented some of these songs as Shannon sang them during the interview. But the discussion developed and also covered the extraordinary work that Shannon and his wife Joan had achieved for the mentally disabled of Montana — as parents of two mentally disabled boys they worked tirelessly to get legislation reviewed and civil rights achieved for this section of Montana's community.

By using a variety of techniques, incorporating the recorded voice, recorded video, sound effects and stage imagery, the actors of *Listen/Éist* brought these various stories to life in front of their audience, some of whom were the storytellers themselves. This script of *Listen/Éist* gives us an insight into the lives of the Montana Irish in their own words and as a shared experience that can be performed in front of a live audience.

My heartfelt thanks to the actors, interviewees, technicians and all who worked to the make *Listen/Éist* possible. Special thanks to co-editor Anna Dulba-Barnett, the funders of *The Gathering: Collected Oral histories of the Irish in Montana, the Irish Government Dept. of Foreign Affairs Emigrant Support Program* and the University of Montana College of Arts and Sciences,

English Dept., Irish Studies Program, the College of Visual and Performing Arts and the School of Theatre and Dance.

Thanks to Consul General Gerry Staunton, *Gathering* Chair Dr. Traolach Ó Riordáin, current project director Bob O' Boyle, colleagues and chair of the School of Theatre and Dance Jere Hodgin, and *Gathering* research assistants John Lovell, Sandy Williamson, and Brandon Woodard. Also thanks to Jerry Fetz and the University of Montana Press, and all who funded this publication.

But, most of all, thanks to all those who have participated in *The Gathering* to date, for allowing us into their homes and their histories.

— *Bernadette Sweeney*

---

[1] For more information on *The Gathering: Collected Oral Histories of the Irish in Montana* go to mtirishgathering.org
[2] For more information on this company and this technique go to www.recordeddelivery.net
[3] This is not intended of course to remind the actor of content, he or she should know this very well at this point, and at a 3 to 5 second time lag it would be impossible to revise content in front of the audience this way — but it is intended to keep the articulation of the material as fresh and as close to the original voice of the interview subject as possible. Schaffer was the only performer to choose to work with this technique and I was very glad she did, as it was intriguing to watch in performance — not quite a sleight-of-hand but a hidden authority at least — which was surprising effective in performance.

LISTEN/ÉIST

Six actors sit facing the audience. A large video screen upstage centre behind the actors. Actors are in black, with minimum use of props and costume to suggest characters.

SCENE ONE

Darkness. Lights rise on Actor 1 as Bob, sitting in a chair upstage. He speaks to the audience.

Actor 1 as Bob Whaley:

My name is Robert (Bob) Whaley. I was born in Missoula on a cold winter day January seventh, 1935. My mother was born in Missoula, my father was born in Stevensville, his father was born somewhere in Minnesota I think and then they came to Montana in 1863. My mother's family was the McNultys from Butte. And so a long Montana legacy as far as my history's concerned. I have a sister Marianne and a brother Kellogg. He died in a plane crash in Chicago in 1979 so we lost him when he was pretty young.

There was no funner place in the world to grow up than in Missoula, Montana in the forties. Four blocks from Mount Sentinel, right across the street from Bonner Park, all the trees that could be climbed were climbed, the back-stop for the tennis court was climbed, leaps were made over the shed they had there for the picnic tables. And then you would have to jump off that roof to the grass, which was about eight feet. I think that's where I learned my, umm, my joy of jumping. Led into my smoke jumper days. I was always able to entertain myself pretty much, but I had a lot of friends in the neighborhood, a lot of kids and I was able to round them up from time to time. Particularly during World War Two when I'd be the Sergeant and I'd tell them we were going to attack Bonner Park and we'd attack across the street and do firing maneuvers across the park. We would charge through the pool that had water in it — doesn't have water in it now, they got those sprinkler systems, but if we got to the other end of the park without losing anybody we were…we were victorious. We would beat the Japanese and the Germans and we defended Missoula, Montana and particularly Bonner Park.

SCENE TWO

Actor 2 as herself, Leah Joki, portraying four generations of her family:

(Actor 2 is sitting on stage, rocking as if in a rocking chair.) I am Leah Marie Joki. I was born and raised in Butte. This is my grandmother, Ann Cecelia Kinsella Backstrom, aka Old Grandma, *(gestures to screen on which appears video of Leah's grandmother Ann Cecelia Backstrom:)* We think she was born in 1901. She passed in 1989. This is the beginning of Four Generations. *(Leah puts on a pair of glasses like those worn on a video image of her grandmother on the screen behind her. Leah's rocking motion mirrors that of her grandmother on screen.)*

Leah Joki: Okay... so Grandma?

Ann Backstrom: What?

Leah Joki: Tell us where you were born?

Ann Backstrom: Up in Walkerville.

Leah Joki: And what was Walkerville like back then?

Ann Backstrom: Oh... it was a little town like... Walkerville was. A little town like out in Basin. I was born up in there and they called it "Chicken Flats."

Offscreen Voice: Why did they call it that?

Ann Backstrom: 'Cuz everybody had chickens and stuff like that. They called it "Chicken Flats."

Leah Joki: How many kids were in your family?

Ann Backstrom: There was... I raised eight. I had nine. I raised 'em all like... they were pretty good kids! Then when they got bigger they all left me! They said "We're through hangin' around. We're gonna' go. Goodbye!" Marty left me when he was seventeen years old... 'go cowboyin'. Got bucked off a horse and his father brought him home on a... on a whatcha' call 'em... on a flatbed truck! *(She laughs)* We thought he broke his back. *(She laughs)* What? I tell ya'... them are the days of real sports, honey. How about that?

Offscreen Voice: Sounds great.

Leah Joki: So how many kids in your family? In...your own family?

Ann Backstrom: How many my mother had? Fourteen she was crazier than hell. *(She laughs.)* I'm the baby of the family. *(She pauses... then she points with her index finger.)* And the only one livin'. My father was Italian... my mother was Irish. So you see... I'm a ... I'm a "Duke's Mixture." *(She laughs)* 57 Varieties! They were born in the olden country. They come over on a boat. *(She smiles)* They didn't have 'em like they got 'em now, you know. Fancy boats and ships and what have ya'. They had an old tug boat' comin home on it. Well they really liked it. Better than they did in the United States. You know.

Leah Joki: So Grandma, how old were you when you got married?

Ann Backstrom: I was sixteen years old and a goddamn fool. If I had to do it again, I would never get married.

(Video of Leah's mother Jeanne Tanner):

Jeanne Tanner: I'm Jeanne Backstrom Joki Tanner. I was born... in Butte Montana, raised here and lived here most of my life, in fact all of my life. Umm...when I was younger I lived up in Walkerville by my grandmother... Kinsella...which was my mom's mother. And I had a lot of wonderful times. Oh well... Meaderville was... umm...where the Italians lived, well Butte was mostly segregated. Meaderville was mostly Italian and they had all these nice Italian restaurants. And to this day a lot of these women still get together and have their big... I guess you'd call it a banquet with the Italians raised in Meaderville. And then, see, when I was growing up Centerville and Walkerville were mostly Irish and English. The Westside, well... that was the elite part of town. Then... Eastside was all Finlanders. And the flat, well the flat like when we moved out here my Uncle Terry said to my mother "Are you moving to Whitehall? What do you want to move out here for?"

(Video of Leah's sister Kris Joki Roberts:)

Kris Roberts: My formal name is Kristine Ann Joki and I was born... in Butte on June 14, 1951. And the oldest of 5 children and my mom and dad and, well, what else? *(She laughs)*

Leah Joki: Sooo.. growin' up in Butte ... umm...were you Irish enough to get by?

Kris Roberts: Oh umm... well in Butte everyone was Irish or if they weren't they were especially Irish on St. Patrick's Day! *(She laughs.)* I just remember growing up... livin' in Butte that there was different areas of town that even in the 50's there were still definite groups like there was you know up above, well we were always at Finntown a lot. That was on Park Street. But above there was where Dublin Gulch was. So up north of Park and Granite was Dublin Gulch and over west of town, because there was such a big group of Irish. And then you had Meaderville, which was the Italians ... down ... umm...where the pit is today. And then you had the Serbians in McQueen. I remember always that part of our life that there were different groups all over and then a lot of Chinese lived over by Grandpa Sweeney's which is my husband's family that are Irish over on Main Street by the high school. There were more... the Chinese over in that area, where the Peking is right now. So there was always, even as we were little kids... having that was part of living in Butte and there was just great heritage and pride in heritage of Butte. And, and where everyone came from, their other countries that they emigrated from.

(Video of Leah's grandmother Ann Backstrom:)

Ann Backstrom: *(She laughs.)* You know my, my husband's been a mining man a good many years. Like I say he's got mining claims out in Basin. They want me to know what I'm gonna' do with them. What am I gonnna' do with them? I can't go out and help. Go out and pick all the dirt up. You know... you have to do assessment work on it? How would I get out there? Walk? How could I climb across the... the goddamn crick? Swim? *(She laughs)*

(Video of Leah's mother Jeanne Tanner:)

Jeanne Tanner: Oh... my mother was, rather a character. My mother talked to everybody whether she knew them or not. And she liked, people, my mom had a real good sense of humor. She could tell jokes. Oh, she was really great at it. She was really sharp at comebacks.

(Video of Leah's grandmother Ann Backstrom:)
Ann Backstrom: So that's it. Then you go to these bars and a guy will tap ya' on the shoulder and say "Hi Honey... how ya' doin'?" "Doin' better than that," I said. *(She laughs)* "Would ya' like to marry me?" I said "well I tell ya' what! Let me see your bank book." *(She snorts)* Turned around and looked at me and walked away. *(She laughs and smiles widely)* "Clever old gal" he said. "You are." And then he said... another guy said "well how about me comin' down to your house and stay at your house?" "I ain't shackin up with ya'. You're not shackin' up with me!" I said. "The neighbors will talk about me!" *(She laughs)*

(Video of Leah's mother Jeanne Tanner:)
Jeanne Tanner: Basically ... I had a very good life here. I had a very good job. I worked with Wilson Motors and Barkley Motors and went to work for Joe Roberts at Rock...Roberts Rocky Mountain Equipment, which I spent 43 years with him as his accountant and corporate secretary. In fact when my youngest daughter and son were born I actually worked 'til the day before they were born. Closed up the office on Friday and they were born over the weekend. So sometimes I feel like I'm sort of a pioneer at working because when I worked women stayed at home but I don't regret it. My children all turned out really well... all five of them they all have college degrees and are raising wonderful grandchildren.

(Video of Leah's niece Joslyn Carney:)
Joslyn Carney: My name is Joslyn Ann Roberts Carney. I was born...February 2, 1978 in Helena, Montana and moved to Butte three months thereafter. Recently I was reflecting upon what... how to live a long fruitful life. And I think Grandma Jeanne is just a witness to... she's eighty-.... she'll be eight-seven in January and she still works. She ran for public office, umm... at eighty-four and won in Butte as the Public Administrator. Every day she wears black and so I wear black in ... umm... in honor of her... and pearls. She is ever the beauty of the ball... poised, dignified, strong. I mean I think that I feel so blessed... *(She begins to cry)* to be, umm... to have grown up in a multigenerational family. Umm... to...to have known my great-grandmother, to still have my grandmother umm... I'm thirty-three and to have my eighty-seven year-old

grandmother still such a powerful, powerful part of my life. Umm... and I didn't ever think that I would come back to Montana. Umm... I left here for... twelve years and my husband brought me back kicking and screaming, umm... but now being back here and living in a small community surrounded by family that's a part of my life daily. I just feel so blessed... umm... and I'm grateful that my husband wanted to come back to a smaller community and to be here and be near my family.... umm... that's it.

Leah Joki: We're an emotional family!

(Video of Leah's Grandmother Ann Backstrom:)

Leah Joki: OK Gramma. Here's a question for ya'. Did you ever hit anybody with a frying pan?
Ann Backstrom: No. No. Never done that.
Leah Joki: I thought you hit Grandpa with a frying pan.
Ann Backstrom: Oh... *(She laughs.)* I hit him with a mop! *(She laughs)* Comin' around the corner! I went out one night and I went out and it was late when I come home and he said "I had to get the babysitter," he said. "So to get the kids to bed. They like her better than they did me." I said "Well half the time you're not around anyway." So he got mad at me and chased me around the house. See we had a... like the house in there... you could go all around. So I hid in the corner and he come around and I slapped him in the face with a mop! (She laughs, snorts and laughs) Ohhh... I was a pup on wheels! *(She fusses with her hair)*

(Video of Leah's sister Kris Roberts:)

Kris Roberts: Umm, growing up with our family one thing that was special is that we always had a multi-generational family growing up. And it was especially with my Mom's family. So Grandmother, Old Grandma who we ended up calling and her and our Grandpa Backstrom were always part of our lives. I remember them picking us up from school or picking us up and taking us to dance lessons. And many evenings that we would have dinner. And not a special dinner but just dinner for after school that there would be Grandmother and Grandpa...and our uncle Jim and the five of us kids, and mom and dad, and possibly another friend or two that just floated on through. It was just always this huge multi-generational family.

(Video of Leah's grandmother Ann Backstrom:)

Ann Backstrom: I don't know… life went on. It's still goin' on. And the one… the one part he said to me "How you all gonna' be…" "I'm gonna' be a one hundred years old and I'm gonna' be just as miserable as I am now." *(She laughs)* The miserabler I am… the better I like it. Shit. *(She laughs)*

(Video of Leah's sister Kris Roberts:)

Kris Roberts: She was a spunky old woman and she kept that spunk until the day she died. And we always, umm… just appreciated her just her go-getting attitude and going for it her whole life. She was… she was the one that we appreciated… with just such spunk in her life.

(Video of Leah's grandmother Ann Backstrom: we see the empty table, as Ann and Leah exit. The camera picks them up going up the steps into the house.)

Offscreen Voice: Okay give us a wave.

Ann Backstrom: What? *(They both turn and wave.)*

Offscreen Voice: Beautiful.

SCENE THREE

Actor 1 as Bob Whaley:

(Standing downstage left, Actor 1 speaks to the audience.) That third tour, I flew helicopters and the OV-10. And the primary mission was reconnaissance, going out, looking for the trails, Ho Chi Minh trails and so forth, that came down from North Vietnam. The very Northwest corner was my sector of responsibility. To the West was Laos, to the North was North Vietnam. We were flying over the Khe Sanh Combat Base – Khe Sanh was a very hard-fought battle there in early 1968 – and off to the East there was this mountain that was called Tiger Mountain. About fifty six hundred feet high and always covered in clouds because of the high humidity. And I had a 'backseat', a new young lieutenant who had just extended his tour over there for six more months just so he could fly in the backseat of the OV-10s because he was so impressed with the job that we did for him when he was an infantry officer on the ground with his platoon. *(He moves back upstage and sits.)*

SCENE FOUR

(Throughout this scene a series of photographs of Colleen, corresponding with the text, flashes across the screen upstage. Each remains for 2-3 seconds. Actor 3 talks the audience through these images as if presenting a slide-show. The actor uses the device of listening to the interview through an earpiece while performing it, see introduction footnote 3)

Actor 3 as Colleen Galvin Holzheimer:

(Photos 1, 2, 3, 4.) I didn't know I was an archivist until I started dragging my stuff out. *(photos 5, 6)* Then I find out: I save stuff, and I put stuff... *(photos 7, 8, 9 10)*. My name is Colleen Holzheimer, and... So, I mostly want to focus on, umm, the story of my grandmother *(photo 11)*, because she had a hard life, and I think she was often maligned. There were two lives for women in the west, if they were not married... umm, they were either a prostitute, or they might've been lucky enough to be a housekeeper or have a boarding house, umm, but, very, umm, ill treated, umm, very poor, they died very young, umm, and it was not a world for women to live it.

A severance came out of Castle.... I can only imagine what an effect it had on her... I'm speaking about her mother... Her mother was Ellen Murphy Stuart... Ellen came with her two daughters came to Castle Montana with her other family members, who were Dwyers, and, umm, *(photo 12.)* I have a picture here that's quite pixilated, because I can't get the,

©Photographs by Rebecca Schaffer/*The Gathering*

umm, original copy of it... but this picture was taken in... let me reference my source, here, so I say it correctly... in 1897, in Butte. But, this photograph was taken in 1897... This picture was taken in 1897, so my grandmother is pictured  here with her biological sister, Meme, and along with her in this picture are two boys, and they are actually her first cousins, they are, umm, James and Neil... or Cornelius, known as Neil... Dwyer. And by this time, my Grandmother would be... I would say here... umm, six years old, and she had, umm, a tragic thing happen to her. She had a minor eye infection, and the doctor she was taken to put some drops in her right eye, which totally destroyed her eye... destroyed the eyeball, so she was told as a child, anytime she was in a picture that she had to turn her head and only get a profile picture, because they didn't want to see that bad side of her face, as it were. In the 1900 Census, it, umm, it was really shocking to me when I found out that my great grandmother had given my grandmother up to other family members, (to the Dwyers), and, I have a hard time reconciling with that decision of hers, and, umm... I knew that they'd lived in extreme poverty. I knew that the men in Ellen's life were underground miners, and were at the bottom of the working rung. I understand that.

So, another thing popped into my mind, knowing the mentality of society, in the late 1800s, if anybody had any kind of a defect at all, they were not looked upon very favorably, so I'm wondering as Ellen Stuart is moving off to Butte, with another man, James Leary, if, umm, James, or, even her mother, didn't feel that Margery was good enough material to go with this new family to Butte. Umm, her... their mother took the older girl, Mary Agnes, Meme, and moved to Butte, and in 1897, married James Leary. She knew her mother

before she left Castle, yet she was forced into this other household, and, umm, that's one of the most difficult things for me to understand, is, umm, number one, how can a mother give up a child, particularly her youngest child at the time, and number two, how do you function in a community and a society, and a family, and not claim that child as your own, and say that it belongs to someone else, almost incomprehensible to me. But as my mother, my own dear mother pointed out to me, things that went on at the turn of the century, and even through depression years... umm, are unthinkable to us today, but people did what they thought was right to survive in their society at the time.

But, needless to say, my grandmother grew up and went on to have a family of her own, and survive still further hardships in her adult life, umm, but still, umm, a joyful spirit, a happy person, and, umm, brought down great traits into her surviving generations today, so for that we can be grateful.

(photo 13) My Grandmother now, has married Frank Galvin, Her marriage to Frank Galvin... I'm pretty much convinced that, umm, my grandmother was... like a slave... in the Dwyer household, she was held responsible for the running of the house, for seeing that they boys were ready for school, umm, she then had to work packing lunches for the miners, I think apparently in Butte, at the time, there was a practice that households would, put lunches together for the miners to take underground, umm, particularly those that lived

in boarding houses that didn't have anyone to do that for them, and how they were paid for that, I'm not sure, but I think that's a practice that took place, and, now, we're into, umm, the early 1900s, 1908, 1909, my grandmother is 18 years old, and it is time for her to be out of the household, the Dwyers have to see that she's married, and, so, within the Irish society, in Butte, they, are acquainted with a lot of the other families, and I'm sure all of the families are looking for suitable partners for the single women, they're still arranging marriages. They're still, umm, making them marry within their nationality, to marry someone Irish, so in the *Anaconda Standard*, Sunday morning, November 1909, an article *(photo: 14)* was printed in the society section, umm, titled 'Pleasantly Surprised', and it says, "a number of friends pleasantly surprised Miss Margie Dwyer at her home, 241 Gordon Ave, last Monday evening, the occasion being her 17th birthday".

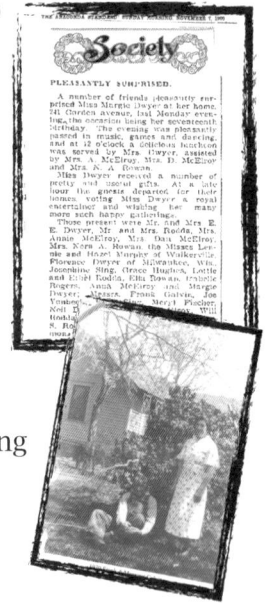

This was her attempt to marry my grandmother off… Mr. Frank Galvin was invited to this party… this was her 17th birthday, *(Photo 15)* Frank was a 29 year old railroad engineer, so he's quite a bit older than my grandmother, and I'll say this, honestly, and my family members agree: our grandfather was a drunk; an alcoholic. He, umm, was fired from the railroad several times for being drunk on the job; he drank what are called boiler-makers, umm, shots of whiskey, umm, with a beer back, and, umm, not one beer, or two, but many. I think he liked to gamble, and I'll show you a picture of my grandmother's wedding rings, and Frank used to use those rings to help him in his gambling endeavors, *(photo 16)* This is the world that my grandmother came out of, and just the fact that she's a survivor, and, umm, that I have this great tradition to follow on, I think is remarkable, and worth remarking upon.

SCENE FIVE
Actor 1 as Bob Whaley:
(*slowly circling stage to end downstage right,*) I was always envious, or I honored, I guess you could say, the Navy and Marine pilots in the Pacific flying off of carriers. I'd see *Flying Leathernecks* or *Helldivers of the Navy* or some movie like that and come home and I'd...I was 9 or 10 years old, I'd get in my father's 1939 Chevy parked out there in the driveway and I'd get in a dogfight, and I'd be shooting down zeros and then I'd bail out of the car into the caragana hedge and proceed to escape and evade through the neighborhood stealing apples and pulling carrots out of people's gardens without being detected. And then make my way home after about an hour and a half of all that all by myself. And the folks would wonder, 'why won't he eat his dinner?'

SCENE SIX
(*Darkness. In the darkness we hear the sound of an 1850s emigrant ship, the pleasant hum of men in a bar, the whistle of a train, its engine bell clanging, and its steam release, the play by play of a 1940s Red Sox game. These are the sounds of Jim's grandfather's life. They stop, the lights begin to rise revealing a figure.*)

Actor 4 as Jim Bullock:
(*handles a cigar throughout this scene*) I'm Jim Bullock and I was born in Bozeman, Montana in ... My great grandfather McMahon, umm, came over from Ireland, umm, about, umm I think they started over here aft... just before the American Civil War, probably 1850 or so there was umm, kind of a second famine in Ireland and there was a second wave of Irish men that came over at that time. (*We hear the sound of a ship...*) And, umm, they were heading for, umm, as far as I know they were heading for Canada. So when they took the boat and came over and they weren't the old coffin ships like they, the earlier Irish that came over, died, terrible fate on those coffin ships but this was fairly decent, but I think one of the interesting things was they came up the St. Lawrence River and were crossing into the Great Lakes when my grandfather was born on the ship and then according

to... his... stories, umm, he had, umm, dual citizenship between Ireland and, 'cos he wasn't in Canada and he wasn't in the United States so he had a, enjoyed a dual citizenship with, umm, from Ireland and from, umm, the United States. Umm. *(Ship sounds die away.)* And, umm, as he grew up, his stories were that he came into, umm, Montana and worked on farms and ranchers and claimed he was a pretty good cowboy, and wound up around, umm, Utica, when, umm, Charlie Russell was a young guy.

So he and Russell got pretty well acquainted, and that acquaintanceship lasted, umm, until Russell died. Matter a'fact down in, umm, Great Falls there was, umm, is a bar, it's gone now, but it was called the Mint Saloon *(We hear the hum of the bar men talking under following monologue throughout...)* right down on Central Avenue, lower Central Avenue, and that's where they would kinda congregate and go into that watering hole, I guess both of 'em were pretty good men with a glass, so they enjoyed each other's company. Years later I, umm, my grandfather'd come down from Havre and pick up my brother and myself and, we were just little guys, I think we were maybe seven, eight, nine years old, umm, we, our home in Great Falls was not very far from the Mint Saloon, so he would walk us down, take us with him, and we would go down to Central Avenue and go in the saloon, full of guys drinking and smoking cigars, and, and jabbering away and they would have a couple of high-balls and they'd give, we'd sit up at the bar and have Seven Up and then we'd trundle on back home. And, umm, what I remember about that mostly, is the umm, well the cigar smoke for one thing, umm, but also the Russell paintings that were up on the wall behind the bar, the back bar there in the Mint. So that was, umm, he was an interesting guy like that. *(The hum dies away.)*

He umm, he went on to do some cowboying but then his, the next thing that I know about him is that he got on the umm, started working for the railroad for, umm, Jim Hill, who was known later as Big Jim Hill, who was a competitor of the Northern Pacific Railroad. It was a pretty big deal. And of course they'd haul wheat and stuff. So he got a job there as a you know, as a gandy dancer, and day laborer and eventually he became a, umm, engineer on one of the, one of the lines. And when he did that they moved him to, umm, from, to Glasgow. And so they lived in Glasgow. My mother remembers living in Glasgow, umm at that time, this was about, oh gosh, before World War One and it was umm, pretty se- pretty severe climate, pretty stark, umm, the Indians still roamed around there in bands, and she said she remembers they were pretty hard up Indians by that time they were on reservations having a tough time, but any rate that's where they lived. And then, umm, he married a, young lady that they brought over from Norway of all places, umm to work on the railroad. As a, umm, Gibson Girl, serving sandwiches and things on the train. Umm and eventually they had oh, five children. They had three boys, my uncle, these all have biblical names, my uncle Abraham was the oldest boy, the second son was Samuel, and the third son was Matthew. I don't... if they'd had a couple more it probably would have been Mar...Matthew, Mark, Luke, and John. Because my grandfather was a very, a, umm, a devout Irish Catholic, by the way. So they had many kinds and then the two daughters, my, my aunt Gene, Genevieve, and my mother, Mary Elizabeth. And umm, so they lived out on that prairie while he was railroading. That was really tough on his wife too, because she would be left alone for days and days out there, and umm, it was really really hard on her, and she didn't last too long. My mom, and Genevieve, and then the two young boys, Sam and Matthew, who became known as Mickey, wound up in the umm, matter a fact the grandmother had passed away, and then she, they had, he had to put the kids down in the St. Thomas Orphans home in Great Falls. Now my grandfather was pretty much an uneducated man but he ad... he admired education, and he wanted all of the kids to get a good education. So what money they had, he made pretty good money on the, on the railroad, he, umm, sent 'em to school.

So, my next big memory of him, almost my first memory of my grandfather was when I was about three years old, well, I was three years old, and they had a pretty good sized earthquake in Helena. And it umm, scared everybody, knocked buildings down, destroyed the hospital, and, and umm, our little house fell apart, so we had no place to live, so they, there was a spur line from, a railroad line, from Havre down to Great, to umm, Helena. And, umm, she packed up all the kids, my dad had to stay and work, help clean up, but she packed us up and we packed on that train at, late at night, (*We hear the sound of a steam engine and jangling chains...*) and I'll never forget the clanging of the bell of the engine, the steam release and then the red light of the, of the umm, conductor, waving their light and we pulled out of the station and then, umm, I rem... I remember my uncle puttin' us on the, the train we went to sleep and then we lived for the next, almost the next year up in Havre, till my dad got a better job. (*The sound of train dies away...*) So that kind of, umm, that was really interesting living with him up in Havre, and I can still see scenes of Havre in the wintertime.

I guess he was a pretty rough and tumble engineer, and, umm, he had two claims to fame that I, that I know about that he would tell us about, umm, one of 'em was he, they had a silk train that ran from Minnesota to Seattle, and they called it the silk train and they would run that line and they would have to go as fast as they could to pick up the worms or whatever it was in Seattle and then get 'em back to Minnesota, and they were silk worms and it was quite a deal. So, umm, ole grandpa, he set the record for the fastest line, the fastest route, the time that, the, that the silk train established and I think it stood until the steam engines went out, and the, and the, umm, diesels came in. But he was, he was quite proud of that and, and the other one was, he was... nothing would hold him back, he was very bold, always had a cigar in one corner of his mouth, talkin' out of the other corner of his mouth. (*Actor does the same with cigar.*) He was, umm, running a line down there in the, in Eastern Montana, and they came to one of the big trestles, and in the middle of the trestle was an Indian woman. I guess, umm, she figured her day had come and she was sitting out in the middle of this really high trestle, with very little side board on it beside the train, and hoping that the train would run over her. So, he hit the brakes and stopped the train, backed it up, and then walked out on the trestle, and she wasn't goin' to move, but he got the conductor and himself and they fin-finally got her off that trestle. So they spared her life.

He, umm, after he retired, he would, umm, come down from

Havre all the time to see my brother and I, my brothers, my older brother Jerry and myself, my sister Dorothy, and the younger brother Tom and he would come down to see us, umm, oh, about once a month, he'd hop the train and this was after he'd retired even, he would just, when we lived in Helena he rode to Helena, and when we lived in Great Falls he would ride it down to Great Falls, and he'd always get the engineer to stop right by Gibson Park, I think you know where that is, and umm, we didn't live far from Gibson park, we lived down on third street on North in Great Falls. And he would say "Stop the train, I gotta get off here." And then he'd hop off the train and then... he was fairly old at this time and he would slide down the side of the railroad embankment and crawl up the Milwaukee line 'cos there were two lines there, the Milwaukee and the Great Northern and then here he'd come. And I remember, umm, early in the morning, we'd still be asleep, and he would come up and, come in the back, open the gate and come in the back yard come up and we were sleeping downstairs, my younger brother and I, and we'd hear "tap, tap, tap" on the window, "tap, tap, tap." It was grandpa, there out there, sun just coming up, and he had the ole' cigar in his mouth. "Lemme in," he'd say, "it's cold out here!" He'd come in there and he was... he was fun to be with.

Umm, there was often times, there was a little tension between my father and my, umm, my grandfather. You know my father was kind of a he was a, umm, his parents had come from England. So, at that time the English and Irish did not get along at all. And umm, boy, I, they would, there was a lot of conflict there. So... But they managed to survive one another, and umm, my dad was pretty much a patient man and he let a lot of stuff go. But umm, he, and he even you know one of the things when umm, when my mother married my dad you know, Catholic, my grandfather insisted that we kids would be raised as Catholics. So we had to go through the whole business and go to the Catholic school and be altar boys and be in the choir and everything. And umm, I, that thing always amazed me, he was so rough and tumble but when he was in church he was just saintly. And very, very polite to the, I was always afraid that he was gonna embarrass himself and us by using foul language in front of the nuns and priests but that would have never happened. But he, umm, he passed on when he was eighty six up in Havre and, umm, I remember it was, the last time I really visited with him was in 1946, *(The play by play of a 1940s Red Sox game is heard underneath and throughout...)* I remember this 'cos I was a kid, the baseball season was on and the Boston Red Sox were gonna' play in the, in the umm World Series that October we were going up there and he was pretty sick then. We listened to the ball game and umm, that was about it. That was about the last time I ever saw him. *(The ball game dies out...)* That's about it. If there's anything else, I forgot. That's it. So... mostly it's true.

(The lights begin to slowly fade. We hear the same sounds as prior. Blackness.)

SCENE SEVEN
Actor 1 as Bob Whaley:

(Sitting.) Peter Whaley came to this country in 1841. And he left the rest of the family in Ireland until they could get enough money to come... which he would send them. And they came about 1847. I think there were six kids in the family. The one I'm most familiar with is my great-grandfather Peter who was the son of the other Peter Whaley. So my great-grandfather came here about 1847 with the rest of the family. And he came from County Carlow. Tullow. Buck Whaley was a great-great-great Uncle. A really ne'er-do-well guy. He was a gambler, never married, probably see why. *(He stands and walks downstage in a circle throughout the following.)* Made a bet with a guy one time that he could walk all the way to the Holy Land. And he got on a boat and walked the whole time he was on the boat they said. I can't believe it, but he hiked on the boat, walked on the boat going across the English Channel, walked across Europe and then across the Mediterranean I guess — probably a small part of it — and walked the whole time he was on the boat there and he won the darn bet.

(He arrives downstage near a small pile of little flat river stones.)

There's a lot of pride in being Irish. As there is a lot of pride for Italians to be Italian, Germans to be German, Swedes to be Swedes, Norwegians to be Norwegians. *(He kneels by the stones and begins stacking them, beginning with the largest and working his way up.)* I think if you're fortunate enough to have enough of a country's blood in your background and it's been foisted upon you or you've had a chance to learn a little bit about it, there's an interest there if you take it. And if you want to pursue it, that, to me, is something to have some pride in. I mean, we're all mongrels, there's no doubt about that. We're all mongrels to a very large degree, but if you can break out the thoroughbred a little bit and put your money on that then why not? *(He balances another rock on top of the stack, leaving some un-stacked, and heads back to his seat upstage.)*

SCENE EIGHT

Actor 5 as Johanna Prindiville[1]:

(Darkness. In the darkness we hear the recorded voice of interviewee Johanna Prindiville:)

Recorded Voice:

My name is Johanna Prindiville, my maiden name was Scanlon. I was born in a place called Ballydorgan in County Cork, Ireland on August 26th, 1935. Okay.

(In the spotlight we see Actor 5 as Johanna. She is sitting comfortably in a chair. She holds a decorative teacup full of tea, which she sips every now and then through the whole monologue.)

Actor 5 as Johanna Prindiville:

June 21st 1947, the longest day of the year and a very hot June 21st. We flew out of Shannon airport in the west of Ireland, arrived at Logan Airport to a massive parking lot. I've never seen so many cars in my life. I remember that particularly that my aunt where we had dinner had tea roses in her garden and I was so relieved because we had only seen pictures of cities without a blade of grass. So that was very comforting. I was eleven at that time. I turned twelve that August, so, almost twelve. When you're eleven it's very important to be almost twelve.

---

[1] The actor playing Johanna Prindiville needs to speak in a warm, calm and friendly manner. Even the most sad and painful memories ought to be delivered with a calm smile. There is no room for bitterness, anger or overt sadness.

(Lights dim slightly. We hear Johanna's recorded voice. During that time Actor 5 as Johanna sips her tea.)

Recorded Voice:
My father was a widower. My mother and infant brother were buried in Ireland. He was left with four children, the youngest of whom now lived in America. She was brought to America by an aunt and uncle. And there were three in Ireland, we lived with different relatives who cared for us and we were separated and that was very painful for him without a home and family.
(Lights up.)

Actor 5 as Johanna Prindiville:
1947, World War Two had finished, United State opened up immigration to northern Europeans and he took advantage of that to collect his three surviving children in Ireland and bring us to America where he hoped that we would live close enough to my baby sister Angela; that we would all grow up knowing each other and knowing him. He didn't... couldn't quite tolerate being so separated. So we came here and it was the land of hope.

We didn't have a home. Immigrants. I had an aunt Nell, who was a widow herself with three children and she took my brother Patrick because she had her son Tom. And my sister Mary and I were lodged in a boarding school, a convent school, an orphanage, a home for homeless girls... whatever you choose to call that. It was operated by the Catholic Church and run by the sisters of Saint Joseph and there we were supervised, fed, taught and lodged for two years until my father decided to marry my aunt Nell. And then we move into a home which she owned in Summerville and became part of the blended family, long before that expression became popular. Yes...

I was so relieved to get out of that boarding school. *(She laughs)* We were the strange ones, we talked funny, our ears were pierced. It was something that the girls we lived with never saw before and so it was good to poke fun and it was a bit like an initiation and then it wore off. They'd push you in the corner and poke you in the chest and they'd say "say something, say something," and then they'd laugh... that's what youngsters do... *(she laughs)* But there was no alternative and this was something my father could afford.

He at that time was referred to in America as a common laborer but I always objected to the word common. I thought there was nothing common about this man. I thought he was quite remarkable but he was a laborer all his life.

I was lucky. I didn't realize it for a very long time that I had come to this country as white, English speaking, healthy and happen to land in the place where Irish immigrants and Irish Americans dominated. So in a sense, umm, I had to stop complaining and consider how difficult it must be for people who did not have those advantages.

I was fourteen when my parents married. I call my mother mom; she was my mother for thirty-seven years. That entitled her to the... mom. She came to this country when she was 18; she was my mother's sister so my mothers were sisters. And because they were next to each other in age, they married around the same time, so their children were all about the same age so that my new sister Patricia or Pat was just one month older than my brother Patrick or Pat. *(She laughs)* Maureen, my new sister was 5 months younger than me and I had a sister then called Maureen so we changed her name to Mary to keep them straight and we retained our surnames. Yes. We still confused a lot of people but they got over it. *(She laughs)*

You asked about my mother, my second mother Nell... Nell was one of 10 children, my mother Nora being my birth mother was buried in Ireland and six of her siblings immigrated to America and Nell was one of them. So she came at a young age, 18, and was well assimilated by the time we met her. So she would be more Boston Irish and we would be considered Irish-Irish. Nell's children and the Scanlon children, we had distinct differences in the beginning because of the cultural differences with which we grew up. Americans tend to be far more assertive than Irish children of that day. They were physically more mature, they seemed to be afraid of nothing. And we were at that time, I think it's safe to say, afraid of almost everything.

(Lights dim slightly.)

Recorded Voice:

You have to understand first of all that my mother died when I turned 8. Let's see, there were five children at that time, so that was devastating, I think is the only word to describe that, to my father and to us because we were separated and sent to live with relatives and didn't see each other very often. We were lucky to have great relatives, that comes in retrospect again, but the idea that we no longer lived together and that our little house in the village of Ballyhooly was no longer ours, that our school, our friends all of that changed. So those were the sad times.

(Lights up. Behind Actor 5 on the screen we can see a projected photo of a small, Irish country house.)

Actor 5 as Johanna Prindiville:

I was born in my grandmother's house, it, this is that house behind me. And I was born at the time when the country was at peace and glad to have it that way, on the small farm, it was like living in a cocoon. And I have fond memories of that, perhaps they are selective, but I have very fond memories of, didn't know the meaning of fear or loneliness, it was the happy time and my grandmother's house which was small and, some would say primitive, we had a phonograph and people would dance in the kitchen and of course storytelling was second nature because, without the electricity that was what you did on those long winter nights in Ireland and with funny Uncle Jack there was just no cause for concern. We lived in the village after that, until my mother died and then I was handed over to an aunt, a sister of my father's and she and her husband Martin had no children so that gave me a whole lot of freedom. The only downside of that was my father with four children who worked six days a week, plus milled for a local farmer on Sunday morning, had just Sunday afternoons to visit each one of us in turn so we only got to see him once a month and that was too bad because we really liked him. But beyond that I have no complaints, I think of Ireland very fondly. Does that mean I did not like The United States? No, doesn't mean it at all. The United States was an adventure.

(The lights go down completely. The only light comes from the projection of the picture.)

Recorded Voice:

There are four of us. I don't know if you've met Valerie, she's a Dubliner and Eve, the women who just phoned, she's a Dubliner and I was the only Corkman for a long time but I assured them that it takes two Dubliners to equal one Corkman! And then we just discovered Anna who lives in Belgrade and she is from Cork city, so now we're even, we give the Dubliners a run for their money!

(The projection of the picture fades slowly leaving stage in complete darkness.)

SCENE NINE

Actor 1 as Bob Whaley:

(Standing center stage.) So he was my backseat and I was telling him about all this stuff and showing him the different areas I had been flying over for quite awhile — I think it was about eight months at that time. And looking over there, out to the West were low rolling hills going into Laos and nice, big Tiger Mountain out there to the East. And I looked up at Tiger Mountain and of all things: it was clear. No fog, no clouds, nothing whatsoever and I said, 'Lieutenant,' I said, 'You're in real luck today.' I said, 'I've been flying for about eight months, nine months and I have never seen it this clear before. I understand,' I said, 'that there are waterfalls up there and crags and things back in that mountain that hold tremendous majesty and beauty.' And I said, 'Let's go take a look at it.' So, we did, and we flew up there. It was surely everything that we'd hoped to see. Absolutely. *(He walks back to the stones.)* I'd always wanted to fly because we didn't live that far from the old Hale Field, which was where Sentinel High School is now. It was about a ten-minute ride on my bike and I used to go out there and watch the planes take off and land all the time. So, when I was a little kid I thought, 'I don't know if I could ever do that or not, but if I could I'd sure like to give it a try.' So I figured, well, why not? It was probably jumping off the roof of that little shed there in Bonner Park and figuring that there was no way I was going to get out of this thing until I hit the ground, but I'd rather be able to get out and fly around a little bit and see something without having to hit the ground. *(He kneels and stacks a few more stones.)*

SCENE TEN

(We hear the sound of wind, underscored by the scratch of a record. At indicated points the recorded voice of Valerie can be heard by the audience in tandem with the actor's. Again, Actor 3 uses the device of listening to the entire interview through an earpiece while performing it)

Actor 3 as Valerie Danby-Smith:

My name is Valerie Danby-Smith. I was born in Dublin, in, May, ... 1940, 5th of May, 1940, *(city sounds of the 1940s play softly.)* I think the world at that time wasn't, umm, wasn't... umm... the way it is now, where everything is judged by how much you have... what you have, acquiring things... the whole fabric of life was... was...it was different, in the sense that, umm, I think the Irish are much more... they're story tellers, and, sort of, umm, fanciful about things, I mean, we had a lot of fairies, and leprechauns were a natural part of existence, umm... not at school, because they didn't come up, umm, that was, umm, I mean, the nuns didn't have any time for that, that was, but... I, I know that fairies ... you, you know... if things were missing... or, you couldn't find something in general, it had something to do with a fairy having moved it from one place to another, or something in your behavior. *(Sounds of outdoors in countryside play softly)* I mean, there were a lot of things like that that had... and that was more country, because I did spend my holidays, not in Dublin, but in County Wicklow, and so that, was, which was closer to the land, and, umm, so, definitely, there were lots of tales of fairies, and fairies are mischievous people, but not, I mean, I think here we think of fairies being pretty and nice. *(Magical sounds effects play softly)* They were not nice... they were very ugly and unpleasant people, and the thing is, you had to be very, nice about them, because otherwise, they could, umm, do things to you, and..., I mean, *(The voice of Valerie can be heard by the audience, Actor 3 speaks in tandem,)* they were called in Irish, er... Irish, certain... er, umm, *Sidhe (shee)*... the, the the fairies, called the good people, and umm, you had to call them the good people, because you knew they were bad, and if you called them bad, then bad things would happen to you.

So, there's that so, there's a lot of fanciful stuff that, that could… was a part of life, and it was nothing to do with children, it wasn't children think that, it was actually adults thought that much more, I mean, children were more likely to say, gosh, I don't believe that, the way of… children will say, I don't believe in Santa Claus, you know, but all of… but everything had a… in… there was a logic to it, and, umm, I mean, for instance: Santa Claus wasn't Santa Claus, because of… I mean, Santa Claus the original Santa Claus …, you know it's, Saint Nicholas, so it was Saint Nicholas bringing gifts. It wasn't this imaginary man that does he exist or doesn't he exist, of course saints exist, and if you're good, you get gifts… you get present, and, you know, there was a logic to it, it wasn't… now things have come in this… we've lost touch with the roots and the roots of, of sort of, the stories of… of who we are, I think, and that, part of that is big cities, *(city sounds of the 1940s play softly.)* I think it happens in cities, but it also happens in, when we have a whole work a day life, and we, we work hard, and then with our money, we go out and we buy stuff, and then our places are absolutely stuffed with all of these objects, and whereas we didn't have any of those things, so we spent endless hours in the, *(sounds of winter weather play softly,)* the winter evenings, *(sounds of a crackling fire play softly)* sitting round the fire, telling stories, and if there was a, as there was… you never told the same story twice, you invented… you just invented… there was no thing, and everybody joined in the invention, you know it wasn't a story that was told over, it was that you used your imagination to build on it. So, whether it's a noise *(sounds of a ticking clock play softly)* or whether it's a clock ticking, or a mouse suddenly appearing from a hole, *(sounds of a shuffling mouse play softly,)* it, you know, all of those things would get together, and then all of a sudden, you're, you're … everybody joins in the story…

I just remember *(sounds of a crackling fire play softly)* watching the flames, the the turf didn't, umm, it was very slow burning, but sometimes it was very cold, we put some anthracite or coal on top of it, and then you have some lovely flames, and then the creaking *(sounds of wind play softly)* and you had to be very close, and… by the fire, because the houses of course weren't heated at all…I mean the house that I grew up in, actually, umm, was built... a beautiful Georgian house, it was built in 1802, and had for a century belonged to the family of a great writer, umm, Joseph Sheridan Le Fanu, and all sorts of wonderful people would have been at that house, *(sounds of people socializing play softly.)* Oscar Wilde's dad would have been there, Bram Stoker would have been there, I mean, it, it, the house had immense history, and it was a beautiful, a beautiful building, and it was an absolute treasure to grow up in, you know, to have that, and to know, to understand, you know, to understand who had been here, you know, the... umm, I mean, Bram Stoker wouldn't have written *Dracula* there, but he, he certainly would have talked about it, and, and, might've got some ideas. But, umm, so, that, you know, when the *(sounds of wind play softly,)* wind whistled through as it did, there were lots of... there were lots of ripples of noises, and, and they made you think, they made you think, and they made you fantasize, and this was... *(Valerie's voice can be heard by the audience, in tandem with Actor 3's)* I mean, you couldn't go into any store anywhere in the world, and, and buy the childhood that I had, you know, you you couldn't, and I couldn't give it to my children either, I mean, so in one way, one was under privileged and not growing up with any family or parents, but in another way, I had a life that was richer than you could imagine.

There were... we didn't have toys, and we really... play was not encouraged at all, you know, umm, children... I mean... we didn't... I mean... it's a, it's a whole different thing, you know? When you were home, you were expected to... to work, to do chores, umm, the idea of playing was considered silly, and useless... I don't ever recall having a toy of any kind. We played outside, *(sounds of crackling leaves play softly,)* but you get sticks and stones and pieces of wood, that was it, and you... and you, you know, invent things, so, at school we played with leaves, we made houses in the fall we... swept up leaves and made little houses out of them, and used stones as... it's... items for our house, and a branch of a tree as a sweeper thing. And if you were in the house, I remember sitting down and reading a book was considered... at home... that was considered a great waste of time, you know... so if anyone saw you sitting reading a book, they would say, you know, get up, dust that, bring this, bring in some coal, bring in some... you know, feed the chickens, it was... it... you know, if anyone saw a child sitting down, that was a detrimental things, so you, you had to sort of find a spot where nobody was going to see you.

But, in school...we learned reams and reams and reams of poetry; ... a lot of them... poets... were anonymous, because, because this was, all said... I mean, all of these had been written in the seventeenth and the eighteenth century, you know, under, I mean, it, it was not allowed, the language was forbidden, so there wasn't an Irish... I mean, if you're talking about, in Irish, Antoine O Raifteiri would be one of them, umm, trying to *(Valerie's voice can be heard by the audience, in tandem with Actor 3's)* think if I can remember one of his... he's got one that's, umm....

Anois teacht an Earraigh
beidh an lá ag dul chun síneadh,
Is tar éis na féil Bríde
Ardóidh mé mo sheol.
Ó chuir mé i mo cheann é
ní chónóidh me choíche
Go seasfaidh mé síos
I lár Chontae Mhaigh Eo.
It's a... spring is coming... Raifteiri said...
Spring is coming and I'm off on my journey
beidh an lá ag dul chun síneadh...
The, spring is coming, the days are getting longer
ní chónóidh me choíche Go seasfaidh mé...
I'm going to to get on my way, and I won't stop for anything until I reach county Mayo.

I never intended to stay... I never... I never imagined I would stay in America. I found I stayed, because you always think, well you know, I can go home... I can go home...
(The sound of wind can be heard. Lights fade.)

SCENE ELEVEN

Actor 1 as Bob Whaley:

(Lights up on Actor 1 at the stack of river rocks) When I married LaWana, I said, and I was a major at the time, hell I was 33 years

old, I said, 'Don't expect me to fly like a married man. I will always fly like a bachelor.' She says, 'I wouldn't expect you to fly any other way.' I said, 'Good.' After I got back I used to... drive LaWana crazy... rub my feet together like this *(He rubs hands together)*, my soles together, before I'd get into bed because I had to get the sand off. That went on for two years. She'd go, 'Oh, Jeez. There's no sand in this house.' Shook that one. *(He holds up the final loose stone)* I like to collect these round river rocks and stack them like this to keep my dexterity up. See how high I can get them without knocking them over myself. *(He carefully places the final stone on the stack, admires it, and walks back to his seat.)*

SCENE TWELVE

(A single light rises to find a man sitting in a chair on stage. He is aged, crumpled back in the chair, his head lolling slightly to one side. When he speaks, his voice is intelligible but garbled and gruff. From the darkness of the auditorium we hear a live Irish-accented female voice.)

Voice:
So, Kevin Shannon, you were born in Corktown?

Actor 6 as Kevin Shannon:
(*his focus rises to a perceived interviewer*)
I was born at 104 ½ Bell Street, Butte Montana. That was where my mother and father was living. I was born in St. James Hospital.
The Angels were painting a picture,
To be hung on Earth solemn below,
Each one of them was adding a color
From the palette of Summer's rainbow.
"It's finished" they all sang in chorus
"Dear master we hope it will suit.
But we'll leave it to you for the calling."
And God smiled as he whispered, "That's Butte".

That's Butte. I love Butte. And I love the way people treat me. And they allow me to treat them. We are what we are. We're proud of it, but we allow you the same privilege. To be what you are, and be proud of it.

I used to make a lot of money as a kid. Singing in the joints. All the Irish had their own joint, and I knew all the comedies and I knew all the sad songs. On payday night, I'd make all the places, selling paper and singing to them. Give me four bits, I'd go home with four or five bucks to my mother.

Voice:
Would you give the money to your mother?

Actor 6 as Kevin Shannon:
Did you have any chance? She was red-headed just like yourself. She was a tough woman.

Voice:
What age were you?

Actor 6 as Kevin Shannon:
'Bout eight or nine. The boarding houses were great. Just to be around them fellas... more comedy. There was more comedy on the streets of Butte than anywhere. People acting theirselves. Expressing themselves.

Voice:
You knew Happy Downey?

Actor 6 as Kevin Shannon:
(Brightening) I did! Happy Downey worked for my father. Half the town worked for my father, at one time or another. Happy and Sid Bynam were great friends, and both could sing. And Sid done a lot of writing and so did Happy. Of the folklore. The mining folklore. One of Happy's songs was a...

(He *sings gruffly)*
"When I was a miner, I was a hard rock miner,
Up in the Mountain Con Mine
The hashers caressed me
And the chambermaids blessed me
And my contract was paying fine.
I soon grew weary,

My eyes were getting bleary,
My lungs were a-wheezing all the time.
So to dodge the undertaker, I turned to a train maker,
And gave up that god damn mine."

I don't know if he wrote it or not. He used to sing it. He used to sing...
(He begins to sing, but falters) "When I was a miner"... no, no...

(He begins to sing gruffly, but in short progression his age seems to melt away. His voice becomes clearer and more confident and he inflates physically. By the end of the song however, he has reverted to being crumpled in his chair with a gruff voice.)
"He shoed her of copper, with manicured toes
Big brown eyes, with a soft velvet nose
Real long ears that came to a tip
And a big ACM brand was on his left hip
My sweetheart's a mule in the mine
I drive him with only one line.
On the dashboard I sit, and tobacco I spit
All over my sweetheart's behind."

Don't get the wrong feeling there. Miners and the company had a lot of opposition between 'em. The left hip, the brand sat. He was spitting on the company brand. Left hip.
Well, they... I'm losing my train of thought...

Voice:
You got married in Nineteen-Fifty...?

Actor 6 as Kevin Shannon:
...Three. April the 25th

Voice:
And your wife was Joan...

Actor 6 as Kevin Shannon:
Joan Redmond. She's a good woman. I picked well. 57 years.
(He sings gruffly)
"Put on your old knee-britches
And your coat of emerald green.

Take off that hat, my darling Pat
Put on your old Capeen
For today's our golden wedding
And I want them all to know
Just how we looked when we were wed
Fifty-Years Ago."

Did you ever hear it? That's a Kerry Song.

"Way down in County Kerry,
In a place they call Tralee
A fine old couple lived there by the name
Of Kat *(he falters)*
umm...Kate and Pat McGee
There's going to be a wedding...
A golden *wedding..."(trailing off)"*
I forget some of that, but that's how it went.

(Again, he begins to sing gruffly, but his age melts away and he rises to stand.)

"Do you remember dancing
out on the village green?
You held me in your arms, dear Pat,
and called me your Colleen
Your hair was black as raven,
now it's turned to gray,
Come over here, old sweetheart dear,
and this to you I'll say."

(He is standing now, smoothly singing with vigor. During the last line he again reverts back to his chair position.)

"Put on your old knee-britches
And your coat of emerald green.
Take off that hat, my darling Pat
Put on your old capeen
For today's our golden wedding
And I want them all to know
Just how we looked when we were wed
Fifty-Years Ago."

Voice: You're making me homesick now.

Actor 6 as Kevin Shannon:
Bringing a tear to your eye? I'll tell you a story: I started, my wife and I, started most of the things done for the retarded in the state. I don't know if you're aware of that or not. The workshops, the group homes, the... everything. And the degree or the certificate at Eastern Montana. My wife got that. The PKU bill[2], we got that. Well anyhow, it was selfish on our part because we had two boys who were retarded, so we were doing it to create room for them, Kevin and Dan. Kevin was the first, then Jackie, then Ellen, then Danny, then Margaret. ... But anyhow, what was I gonna tell ya?

Voice: The work that you did for the mentally disabled, Kevin, how did you achieve it?

Actor 6 as Kevin Shannon:
Just pure ignorant fighting, fighting fighting. The state would look awful embarrassed taking me to court. You know? That's how it was then. Now, I'm not bullshitting you at all. It just took that and the tear of a mother. Pretty hard to say no to a mother with a tear in her eye. I capitalized on her.

(*His age melts away, he rises from his seat and moves centre to engage directly with the audience.*)

1958. A sailor's wife come to our house. I just can't remember her name. Up on Park Street. And she says, "Some action has to be done. There's no special education, there's no nothing." So she says, "We should form a retarded association." So my wife and I got active and we went out and formed one with Winky Axels and she says, "We gotta' pick an area. Has to be named for the area we're gonna' work in." Well we didn't want to shut anybody out. So we called it the Rocky Mountain Association.

Now we're getting down to where I'm an "I Guy", and I don't like to be using "I, I, I" but for the sake of "I"...
I went to Mr. Mansfield, who was a great close friend of my

---

2 PKU Phenylketonuria is a condition where babies are born without the ability to break down amino acid phenylalanine. The bill brought in newborn screening and treatment in Montana.

father's. I'll tell you how close they were. My father pulled a Johnson button off of Mansfield's coat at a convention in Helena. Said, "Not this time Mike, we're putting an Irishman in." Anyhow, Dr. Westwall called me to Boulder and he had Mansfield's letter, and he says, "Mr. Shannon, come in and sit down. I'm so glad to meet you." Christ, I thought I walked into one of the greatest receptions I was ever at. "I want to show you a list of kids who are waiting to get in here." And he handed me a list of over nine hundred names, and my boy was at the bottom. And I said, "This is what has to be done to create the vacancies. There has to be special education classes, so people can keep their kid at home. There has be sheltered workshops for the older kids. There has to be a nursery." He gave me the list, that was that. So we had to go and change all the laws.

Course, I had a lot of bastards who fought me. Some was an enemy, some was a friendly fight. It was bitter. It was bitter to take and hear the insults about your own kids. And that's what we opened ourselves up to. I got accused of being Jesus Christ. But nobody can say no to a mother with a tear in her eye. And nobody'll condemn you for fighting for some poor individual who can't speak for himself. And that... umm, I'm preaching again. But that's how it was done.

The workshop: I promised them thirty minutes every day. And I'd sell something they could make. The greatest was the surveyor stakes. And it kept them kids busy. God, those kids loved me when they see me. You oughta see those kids when they're working. I had a little kid, I took him into Boulder. His name was Jimmy Hughes. He was in Boulder for forty years. He was put in Boulder when he was twenty-one and he was sixty-one when I got him out of there. He drug this leg sideways and would wear a helmet 'cos he'd have seizures. And that's why they put him in Boulder, 'cos he was having seizures. Nothing wrong with his brain. But he got to reading all the postal forms on Disneyland, they'd advertise it in the leaflets. One day he says to me, "I wanna go to Disneyland." I says, "Do you?" "Yeah." So I says, "Alright, I'll see what I can do." And the Snap E. Tom tomato juice people, good friends of mine, their name was Vujovich. The three brothers give me $300 a piece. So I get a ticket for Jimmy and another little girl that was in with my kid to go June the sixth.

Well, just prior to that I had Mansfield in the workshop going through. And Jimmy Hughes said to him, "Are you Mike Mansfield?" He says "Yeah." He says, "You're the Senator from Montana?" He says, "Yes I am." He says, "You get me my civil rights." And Mansfield says, "What gives 'em?" I says, "Well Mike when there's a commitment made by parents, you lose your civil rights." And Jimmy was committed by his parents. And we had a fight, oh Jeez. Anyhow, Jimmy gets his civil rights. I collected the $900 for Disneyland. I told Jimmy he had to be there June the sixth. He says, "I won't go." I said, "Why the hell won't you go?" He says, "I gotta vote. I got my civil rights. For the first time in my life I can vote." So we had to change the dates. But ain't that something? Guy is 61-years-old and so pleased.
(*With the final line he ages again and returns to his chair*)

Anyhow, he went to Disneyland and had a good time.

Voice:
Well, you've made quite a contribution Kevin.

Actor 6 as Kevin Shannon:
Well, now that's where we are getting into trouble. I didn't tell you that to build myself. That's what this "I" gets me upset. I selfishly done that. I eliminated that list that my kid was nine hundred on. That was the object.

Voice:
Well, good for you. I'm giving you credit for it nonetheless. I don't care how selfish you think you are. You made a big difference.

Actor 6 as Kevin Shannon:
My three girls were my reward for what I done. I'm very jealous for my daughters. Very jealous. And it's from giving those boys up so young. That wife of mine is a tough woman. And those big, beautiful eyes. I wrote a song:
(*He begins singing seated, changes from aged to young in the first line, and reverts to aged during the final line.*)
"Did anyone ever tell you Mrs. Shannon

That your daughters have the nicest eyes of blue?
Did anyone ever tell you Mrs. Shannon
'tis amazing how they look so much like you?
They have your way of smiling
They have your freckled nose
You can tell they kissed the Blarney
Take it from me
They're sweet as can be
You can betcha my life that it shows.
Did anyone ever tell you Mrs. Shannon
That they favor just a bit of their father too
I'm proud of my darlin' daughters Mrs. Shannon
But you're my girl and I'm in love with you!"

Voice:
You're an old romantic Kevin.

Actor 6 as Kevin Shannon:
Nah, *(he chuckles)* she hasn't got a bit of romance in her.

Voice:
Well Kevin, we are wearing you out. We really appreciate your time and your stories.

Actor 6 as Kevin Shannon:
It's been nice. *(Fade to black)*

SCENE THIRTEEN

Actor 1 as Bob Whaley:
(lights up on Actor 1 standing center stage.) There were beautiful rock outcroppings and waterfalls cascading down and...and Lieutenant said, 'Look Major out to our left, nine o'clock low, in the opening in the falls,' he said, 'elephants!' And, the clay out there, the ground is predominantly red clay so they were rolling and spraying themselves so I roll the aircraft abruptly to the left and gaze down on the herd of eight to ten elephants including several calves and one of which appeared to be nursing from its mother. And he says, 'I don't believe it, they're all pink.' And

I told him why because the ground and so forth that they're rolling in and he says, 'Major', he says, 'are we going to shoot them ourselves or are we going to call in an air strike?' And I said, 'Lieutenant, we're not going to do either. No way.' And I said, 'I realize in the hostile sector that we're in here, no known friendly personnel, no known enemy personnel, there are no pack-marks on the backs of these animals', because the Viet Cong and the North Vietnamese would use elephants and water buffalo as instruments of transport for their arms and their ammunition. But there was nothing like that, there was no mark or anything like that on them. No force recon units had reported any activity around that area. These elephants had finally found themselves a respite from the war. They found a place they were safe. 'But Major, we're supposed to.' And I interrupted him and said, 'We're not reporting this and if I hear anyone asking about this or word gets out and some trigger happy S.O.B. goes looking for them I'll have you over to see the flight surgeon and you can explain the pretty pink elephants to which I will personally deny and you'll have your sorry ass grounded.' Or words to that effect. I said, 'Do you understand what I'm saying?' He says, reluctantly, he says, 'Yes, Sir.' And then I said, 'If I thought it would make difference in the war, I'd reconsider this.' I said, 'It's not going to make a darn bit of difference as far as the outcome of this war is concerned. So we're not going to report it. Do you understand?' I said. A formal, 'Yes, Sir,' was the response and we took another pass over them. An old bull was rolling on his back with all four legs in the air. The Lieutenant exclaimed, 'That's just what my dog likes to do.' My point was made and accepted. There was also a calf nursing from its mother. I mean, what more did you ever want to see up there? It was perfect.

(Lights fade as a video of Bob appears on screen — the next sentence is spoken by Bob on video and Actor 1 simultaneously. Actor 1 makes his way to his seat.) Since we didn't always fly with the same observer, it was several days before I saw him again and it was at nighttime. *(Bob reads from a piece of paper on the video as Actor 1 sits in his upstage seat, no longer speaking.)* He was at a table in our makeshift officers' club

and he was sitting with some other lieutenants. And he'd had a few brews, and I caught his eye and he gave me this sly grin and a thumbs-up. I gave him a thumbs-up back. I knew our little pact was honored and our secret was safe. A week later I knew it would be honored forever. He was killed along with his pilot. And I knew his pilot pretty well. At least I hope we let something live on in that war that destroyed so much. And then I added this after I had written this because I thought it was appropriate: "We are defined not only by what we create, but by what we refuse to destroy."

(The lights fade with the video.)

©*Photograph by Bryan Ferriter*

THE GATHERING:
COLLECTED ORAL HISTORIES OF THE IRISH IN MONTANA